Bond
No.1 for exam success

English
Assessment Practice for the 11+

Ages 6–7 Year 2

Sarah Lindsay

OXFORD
UNIVERSITY PRESS

Great Clarendon Street, Oxford, OX2 6DP, United Kingdom

Oxford University Press is a department of the University of Oxford.
It furthers the University's objective of excellence in research, scholarship,
and education by publishing worldwide. Oxford is a registered trade mark
of Oxford University Press in the UK and in certain other countries

© Oxford University Press 2025
Written by Sarah Lindsay
Illustrations © Oxford University Press 2025

The moral rights of the author have been asserted
Database right Oxford University Press (maker)

First published in 2025

All rights reserved. No part of this publication may be reproduced,
stored in a retrieval system, transmitted, used for text and data mining,
or used for training artificial intelligence, in any form or by any means,
without the prior permission in writing of Oxford University Press,
or as expressly permitted by law, or under terms agreed with the
appropriate reprographics rights organization. Enquiries concerning
reproduction outside the scope of the above should be sent to the
Rights Department, Oxford University Press, at the address above.

You must not circulate this book in any other binding or cover
and you must impose this same condition on any acquirer

British Library Cataloguing in Publication Data
Data available

978-1-38-206076-9

10 9 8 7 6 5 4 3 2 1

Printed in China

The manufacturing process conforms to the environmental
regulations of the country of origin

Acknowledgements

Content Development Editor and Reviewer: Anthea Morton
Page make-up: York Publishing Solutions Pvt. Ltd.
Cover illustrations: Lo Cole
Illustrations: Louise Barton, Gemma Hastilow and York Publishing Solutions Pvt. Ltd.

P59 'Slick Nick's Dog's Tricks' by David Harmer from The Very Best of David Harmer by David Harmer, published by Macmillan Children's Books, 2001. Reproduced by permission of the Publisher. P70 Extract from 'George Starts School' by Dick King-Smith from Philbert the First and Other Stories by Dick King-Smith published by Puffin Books, 1996. Reproduced by permission of the United Agents.

Although we have made every effort to trace and contact
all copyright holders before publication this has not been
possible in all cases. If notified, the publisher will rectify
any errors or omissions at the earliest opportunity.

A Brief History of Bond

Bond 11+ has been the market leader in selective school admission test preparation since 1964, when J.M. Bond published her first book of practice tests.

Jean Moyra Bond was a school principal and passionate educator who started writing out practice questions for her pupils on slips of paper, to help get them test-ready, at a time when no formal resources were available. Her high-quality questions spawned a series of books and the Bond range grew from there; however their original author was advised to publish under her initials, rather than her name, as it was felt that the books would not sell as well if it was known they were written by a woman.

Happily, times have changed; but Jean Moyra Bond's legacy lives on, supporting thousands of pupils on their 11+ journey every year. 'J.M.' Bond was involved in writing and revising Bond materials up until her death in 2011, with the baton being passed on to the new generations of expert tutors who create Bond's peerless learning and practice content.

Now offering cutting-edge digital solutions, as well as a comprehensive print range, Bond remains as the gold standard in 11+ preparation to this day.

Contents

Welcome 4
A Note for Parents 4
How to Use This Book 4
English Skills 5

Learning Papers

1 Comprehension and the Alphabet 6
2 Punctuation 12
3 Spelling 16
4 Sentences 20
5 Grammar 1 24
6 Understanding Words 28
7 Making Words 31
8 Grammar 2 35
9 Choosing Words 39
Puzzle 1 42

Mixed Papers

Mixed Paper 1 43
Mixed Paper 2 48
Mixed Paper 3 53
Mixed Paper 4 59
Mixed Paper 5 64
Mixed Paper 6 70
Puzzle 2 76

Keywords 77
Answers A1
Progress Chart A10

Welcome

Bond's English resources provide thorough and continuous practice for key English skills. They are ideal preparation for **Key Stage 1 and Key Stage 2 SATs, the 11+ and other selective school entrance exams.**

Bond offers a complete, flexible programme of preparation materials that you can adapt to your child's specific needs. Bond provides a wide selection of question types and believes that an enriched education is the best preparation. We help children to both master the techniques and develop the logic and rationale to tackle any unknown question types.

KEY STUDY SKILLS

Here are some tips to help:

- Balance short bursts of practice with longer assessment papers.
- Create a quiet study space with pencils, an eraser and paper for working out.
- Limit distractions, such as the television, technology and games.
- Remember that errors are useful. They are part of the journey to success.

A Note for Parents

Parents have a crucial role in helping children and motivating them. Here are some ways that you can really make a difference.

- Check your child is working at the right level. The goal is being able to score 85% on average. It is demotivating if they cannot complete questions.

- Mark their work promptly and go through errors. If papers have not been marked, a child has no idea how they are doing or whether they are repeating the same mistakes.

- Limit the range of homework you give to your child. The best results are achieved by a system that gradually increases in difficulty. Completing lots of books and papers does not guarantee your child's success and often creates stress.

- If your child is struggling with something specific, add additional support in that area.

- Communication is key. Encourage your child to focus on the positive.

How to Use This Book

It is very important that you find the time to work through this book with your child. It is likely they will need support to understand the Key Skill explanations. Once these elements are understood the questions should be more easily accessed by them independently.

This book includes many step-by-step techniques for solving different question types.

- The first section of the book is the Learning Papers that focus on key skills with worked examples then questions for consolidation.

- The second section of the book is Mixed Papers so that children continue to consolidate and do not forget what they have learnt.

- There are fully worked out answers to explain how an answer has been reached.

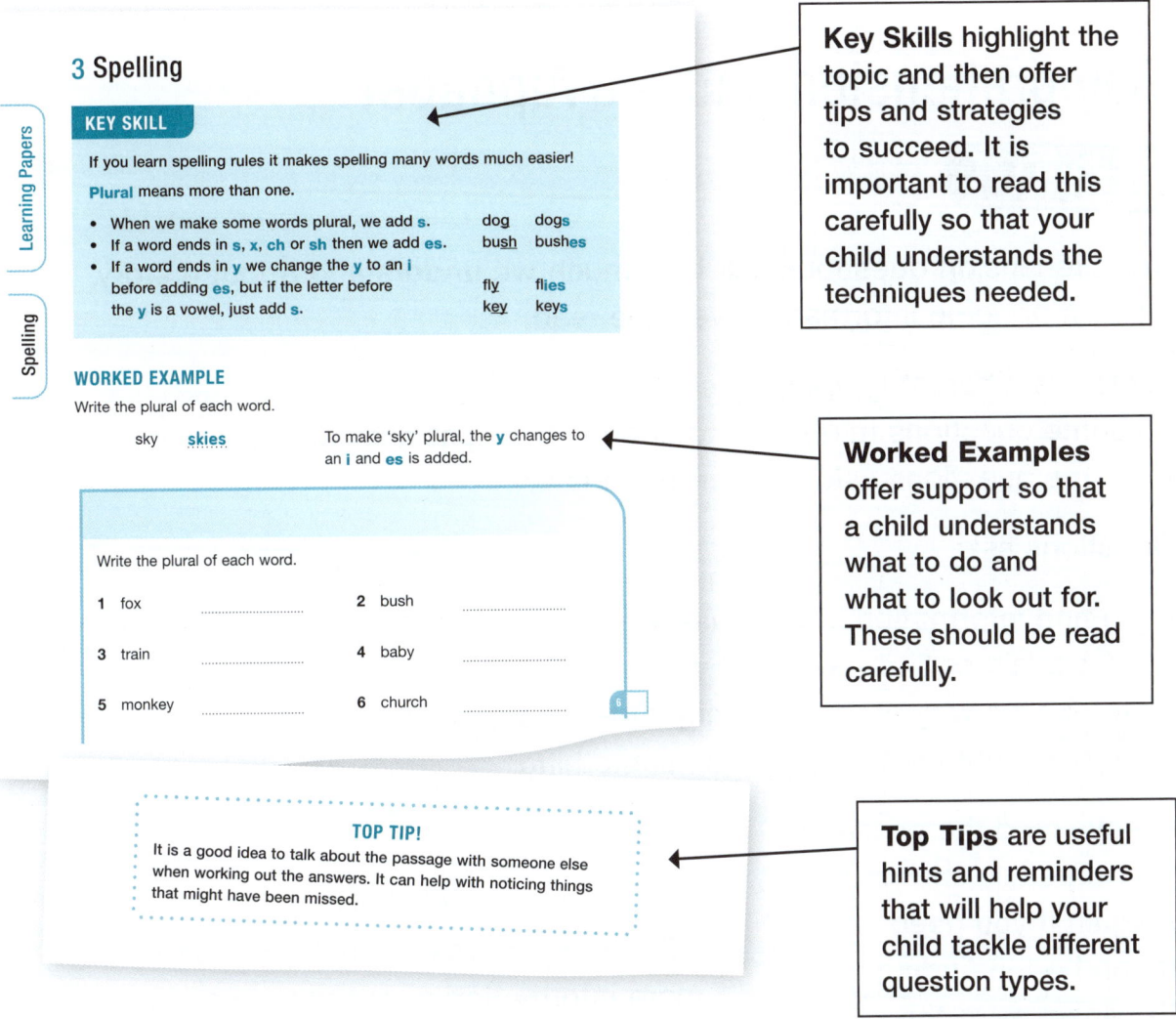

Key Skills highlight the topic and then offer tips and strategies to succeed. It is important to read this carefully so that your child understands the techniques needed.

Worked Examples offer support so that a child understands what to do and what to look out for. These should be read carefully.

Top Tips are useful hints and reminders that will help your child tackle different question types.

English Skills

The Learning Papers cover key skills in comprehension, spelling, grammar, punctuation and vocabulary work appropriate for children of this age. They are fully in line with the National Curriculum for English. One of the key features of Bond Assessment Practice is that children are able to practise a wide variety of skills and question types so that they are always challenged to think – and do not get bored attempting the same question type repeatedly. It helps children to 'think on their feet' and cope with the unexpected.

Do not forget that a rounded education is key.

- Read a range of literature with your child – stories, poems, non-fiction, comics – it all counts.

- Experiencing new places together, such as a visit to a museum or a walk through the woods can stimulate interesting discussions. It also deepens your child's understanding of the world and helps to build essential vocabulary.

- Play games together – card games can develop memory, while word games like Scrabble help with spelling, vocabulary and addition skills.

Learning Papers

1 Comprehension and the Alphabet

KEY SKILL

Comprehension questions ask how much we understand about a story, a poem or some information we have read.

There are different types of question.
- Some questions might ask to choose the right answer.
- Some questions ask for a written answer.

Questions ask:

- to find information in the passage
- to explain or find a word or words
- to explain why something might have happened
- to give your own thoughts on something.

Always read the passage very carefully and read it again if you need to. It can be fun finding the answers to the questions!

TOP TIP!
Often the pictures will help give you more information about the passage so look at them carefully, too.

Read this passage:

Printing with Paint

You will need:

- some thin sponge
- a square piece of cardboard
- a felt-tip pen
- some thick paint
- some glue
- a large piece of paper

1. Draw a simple shape on a piece of thin sponge using a felt-tip pen.

 2. Cut out your shape carefully and stick it with glue on a square piece of cardboard to make a print block. Wait until the glue dries.

3. Cover the sponge on your print block with thick paint. Press the block on your piece of paper a number of times. When the paint on the sponge runs out, you can add more to continue printing.

You can make other printing blocks using different shapes cut out of thin sponge or string dipped in glue and left to dry.

TOP TIP!

It is a good idea to talk about the passage with someone else when working out the answers. It can help with noticing things that might have been missed.

WORKED EXAMPLE

Underline the correct answer.

What type of paint do you need to print with?

    a   **b**   **c**
   thin   <u>thick</u>   does not matter

Thick is the correct answer. In the "You will need:" list it says what type of paint is needed. It says "some thick paint".

Underline the correct answers.

1. What do you draw the simple shape on to?

a	b	c
the sponge	the paper	the cardboard

2. When do you add more paint to the sponge?

a	b	c
each time you print	never	when the paint runs out

3. Look carefully at the list of things you need. Something is needed for instruction 2 but it is missing from the list. What is it?

a	b	c
scissors	a pencil	a ruler

WORKED EXAMPLE

Answer this question.

Why do you need a felt-tip pen?

You need a felt-tip pen to draw the shape on to the sponge.

The first instruction says, "Draw a simple shape on a piece of thin sponge using a felt-tip pen."

Answer these questions.

4 Instructions are written using **verbs**. Write a verb found in this passage.

> **TOP TIP!**
> A verb is a 'doing' or 'being' word. Instructions often start with a verb.

……………………………………………

5 When you stick the sponge on the cardboard you should wait until the glue dries. Why do you think this is?

……………………………………………………………………………………

……………………………………………………………………………………

6 Write what you think you could use your printed paper for.

……………………………………………………………………………………

KEY SKILL

The 26 letters of the alphabet have a special order called **alphabetical order**.

a b c d e f g h i j k l m n o p q r s t u v w x y z

Most letters are **consonants**. Five letters are **vowels** and they are:
a e i o u

WORKED EXAMPLE

There are three letters missing in the alphabet. Which letters are they?

a b c d e f h i j k l n o p q r s t u v x y z

<u>g</u>   <u>m</u>   <u>w</u>

a b c d e f <u>g</u> h i j k l <u>m</u> n o p q r s t u v <u>w</u> x y z

Saying the alphabet out loud makes it easier to hear which letters are missing.

There are three letters missing in each alphabet. Which letters are they?

a b d e f g h i j l m n o p q r s u v w x y z

7 ____   8 ____   9 ____

a b c d e f g h j k l m n o q r s t u w x y z

10 ____   11 ____   12 ____

KEY SKILL

Dictionaries are written in alphabetical order. It makes it easier to find the words.

If it is hard to find a word, write out the alphabet. This will help with seeing the order of the words.

WORKED EXAMPLE

Write the word for the picture. Then write two more words that start with the same letter.

   man   monkey   magnet

The picture shows a man. **Man** begins with the letter **m**. Two more words that begin with the letter **m** are **monkey** and **magnet**.

Write the word for each picture. Then write two more words that start with the same letter.

13  ....

14 ....

WORKED EXAMPLE

Write these words in the order you find them in a dictionary.

| dog | fish | hawk | badger |

1 badger   **2** dog   **3** fish   **4** hawk

When putting words in the order they are found in the dictionary, look at the first letter of each word. It can help to write out the alphabet. Look at where each first letter comes in the alphabet and this will give the correct order to write them.

Write these words in the order you find them in a dictionary.

| nose | mouth | ear | head |

15 ....   16 ....

17 ....   18 ....

Total 22

Comprehension and the Alphabet

2 Punctuation

KEY SKILL

Punctuation helps to understand what has been written.

- A sentence that tells something ends with a **full stop (.)**.
- A sentence that asks something ends with a **question mark (?)**.
- A short sentence, or word, that gives strong feeling ends with an **exclamation mark (!)**.

TOP TIP!

Do not forget capital letters are used at the beginning of sentences and for special naming words like the names of people, the days of the week and the names of places and countries.

WORKED EXAMPLE

Copy the sentence. Add the missing capital letters and punctuation.

shall we go for a walk

Shall we go for a walk?

This sentence needs a capital letter for the beginning of the sentence and a question mark at the end because it is asking something.

Copy each sentence. Add the missing capital letters and punctuation.

1 we are going on holiday

   ....

2 quick, take over

   ....

3 did the dog get the ball

   ....

Punctuation

KEY SKILL

Other punctuation can also make writing clearer.

Commas (,) are used when writing lists.

Commas are placed between the items in a list.

   Ellie likes the colours red, blue, green and purple.

WORKED EXAMPLE

Copy this sentence and add the missing commas.

   The dog likes to eat apples carrots cucumber and dog biscuits.

   The dog likes to eat apples, carrots, cucumber and dog biscuits.

Commas are placed between **apples**, **carrots** and **cucumber** to show these words are part of a list. The last two items in the list are separated by the word 'and' instead of a comma.

Copy these sentences and add the missing commas.

4 Elena loves maths history sport art and science.

....

....

5 Ronan bought bread milk crisps cream and sweets at the shop.

....

....

6 On holiday we travelled by boat car bus train and plane.

....

....

KEY SKILL

Apostrophes (') appear in words to give more information.

- Apostrophes for **contraction** show when letters are missed out of a word.

    she will = she'll   (the **wi** is missing)
    he is = he's   (the **i** is missing)

- Apostrophes for **possession** show when one thing belongs to another.

    pencil belonging to **Arjun** = **Arjun's pencil**

WORKED EXAMPLE

Write a new word using an apostrophe.

I am = **I'm**   The apostrophe for contraction replaces the missing **a** in **am**.

Write a new word using an apostrophe.

7 I will = ...

8 they are = ...

9 he is = ...

10 we have = ...

WORKED EXAMPLE

Write each of these using an apostrophe.

the hand belonging to Tia = **Tia's hand**

The apostrophe for possession shows that it is Tia's hand.

Write each of these using an apostrophe.

11 the pillow belonging to Zola

....

12 the tractor belonging to the farmer

....

13 the scream belonging to Amar

....

3 Spelling

KEY SKILL

If you learn spelling rules it makes spelling many words much easier!

Plural means more than one.

- When we make some words plural, we add **s**.   dog   dog**s**
- If a word ends in **s**, **x**, **ch** or **sh** then we add **es**.   bu**sh**   bush**es**
- If a word ends in **y** we change the **y** to an **i** before adding **es**, but if the letter before the **y** is a vowel, just add **s**.   fl**y**   fl**ies**

  k**ey**   key**s**

WORKED EXAMPLE

Write the plural of each word.

sky   **skies**   To make 'sky' plural, the **y** changes to an **i** and **es** is added.

Write the plural of each word.

1 fox ....   2 bush ....

3 train ....   4 baby ....

5 monkey ....   6 church ....

KEY SKILL

A **suffix** is a group of letters added to the end of a word to change its meaning.

Remember the rules when adding the suffixes **ing**, **ed**, **er**, **est** or **y**.

- If the word has one **syllable**, and ends with **a vowel then a consonant**, the consonant is **doubled** before the suffix is added.

    ru<u>n</u>   run**n**er, run**n**ing, run**n**y

- If the word ends with a consonant + **e**, the **e** is dropped and the suffix is added.

    hi<u>ke</u>   hik**er**, hik**ed**, hik**ing**

- If the word ends with a consonant + **y**, the **y** is changed to an **i** and the suffix is added.

    happ<u>y</u>   happ**ier**, happ**iest**

TOP TIP!

Remember, there are five **vowel** letters: **a e i o u**.
All the other letters are **consonant** letters.

WORKED EXAMPLE

Circle the word spelled correctly.   (**dropping**)   droping

The word **drop** has one syllable and ends with a vowel and consonant, so the consonant is doubled before the ending **ing** is added.

Circle the word spelled correctly.

7	batter bater	8	sadest saddest
9	niceest nicest	10	shiney shiny
11	cried cryed	12	copier copyer

KEY SKILL

If a suffix starts with a consonant letter then it is added to most words without any changes needed.

care + **ful** = careful   enjoy + **ment** = enjoyment

WORKED EXAMPLE

Write the new word.

slow + ly = **slowly**   The **ly** suffix starts with a consonant, so it can be added to the word 'slow' with no changes.

Write the new words.

13 agree + ment = ...

14 pain + ful = ...

15 fear + less = ...

16 sad + ness = ...

17 treat + ment = ...

18 quick + ly = ...

KEY SKILL

A **prefix** is a group of letters added to the beginning of a word to change its meaning.

The prefixes **un** and **dis** change the word to its **opposite** meaning.

happy → **un**happy   like → **dis**like

WORKED EXAMPLE

Add the prefix **dis** or **un** to the word to make a word with the opposite meaning.

........obey   **dis**obey

The word obey means to do as you are asked. It is changed to its opposite meaning by adding the prefix **dis**. **Disobey** means to not do as you are asked.

TOP TIP!

To check which prefix to choose, say the word out loud using each prefix and notice which prefix sounds like a real word.

Add the prefix **dis** or **un** to each word to make a word with the opposite meaning.

19 .... tie   **20** .... agree

21 .... appear   **22** .... trust

23 .... true   **24** .... tidy

Total 24

4 Sentences

KEY SKILL

Sentences must make sense.

There are four different types of sentences.

- A **statement** sentence **gives information** and usually ends with a full stop (.).
- A **command** sentence **tells someone to do something** and usually ends with a full stop (.).
- A **question** sentence **asks something** and ends with a question mark (?).
- An **exclamation** sentence **expresses strong feeling** and ends with an exclamation mark (!).

TOP TIP!

Remember that sentences start with a capital letter.

WORKED EXAMPLE

Rearrange the words so the sentence makes sense.

go to house? Shall we Jake's
Shall we go to Jake's house?

Remember, each sentence starts with a capital letter and ends with a punctuation mark. As this sentence has a question mark, the next step is to look for a question word to start the sentence.

Rearrange the words so the sentence makes sense.

1 have the sweets Where all gone?

   ....

2 at the benches room. Sit down the back on of the

   ....

WORKED EXAMPLE

Write a question for the statement.

> Statement: Sarah had baked beans for tea.
>
> Question: **What did Sarah have for tea?**

The statement gives the subject for the question. Think of a question word to start the sentence. In this example **what** was used.

> ### TOP TIP!
> Question sentences begin with question words like: **what**, **where**, **when**, **why**, **can**, **shall** or **how**.

Write a question for each statement.

3 Statement: Kisha is seven years old.

Question: ....

4 Statement: Tim went swimming after school.

Question: ....

5 Statement: Liam rode his bike to Tayah's house.

Question: ....

WORKED EXAMPLE

Use the picture to write a question.

Is the dog scared of the giraffe?

Use the giraffe and the dog to help you write each type of sentence.

6 statement ....

7 question ....

8 exclamation ....

9 command ....

KEY SKILL

How sentences are written can give us a clue about when something happened.

If an action is **happening now** it is written in the **present** tense.

If an action has **already happened** it is written in the **past** tense.

Think of something that is happening now. This is happening in the **present**.
Can you think of something that happened yesterday or last week? That happened in the **past**.

> **TOP TIP!**
>
> If the action word (verb) ends in **ing** it often means it is happening in the present.
>
> If the action word (verb) ends in **ed**, it often means it happened in the past.

WORKED EXAMPLE

Read this sentence. Write whether it happened in the past or is happening in the present.

Sam worked with Kwame at school.   past

This sentence tells us about something that has already happened, so it happened in the past. A clue is that the action word (verb) ends in **ed**.

Read these sentences. Write whether they happened in the past or are happening in the present.

10 Shona jumped into the puddle.   ....

11 Manjit is flying his kite.   ....

12 Katie walked home from school.   ....

13 Elias is playing the drums.   ....

14 I am learning my spellings.   ....

5 Grammar 1

KEY SKILL

Grammar tells us about words and how they can be put into sentences.

Nouns are words that name a person, place, thing or idea.

There are different types of noun:

Common nouns are the names of ordinary things, like chair.

Proper nouns are the names of people, places, days and months, like Sunday.

Collective nouns are the names of groups of things, like swarm.

TOP TIP!
Proper nouns start with capital letters.

An **adjective** is a word that describes somebody or something. An adjective describes a noun, like kind or scruffy.

WORKED EXAMPLE

Underline the nouns and circle the adjectives.

   tall   Wednesday   hand   tasty

Wednesday and **hand** have been underlined because they are nouns; a proper noun and a common noun.

Tall and **tasty** have been circled because they are adjectives, words that can be used to describe a noun.

Underline the nouns and circle the adjectives.

1 dirty   sausage   long   kite

   herd   America   soft   June

KEY SKILL

A **phrase** is a group of words that stand together as a unit in a sentence.

A **noun phrase** is a group of words that gives more information about a noun in the sentence.

Mr Trevis looked after <u>the scruffy dog</u>.   **the scruffy dog** is the noun phrase

WORKED EXAMPLE

Underline the noun phrase in the sentence.

The sleepy cat slept in the chair.   <u>The sleepy cat</u> slept in the chair.

This noun phrase **the sleepy cat** gives us more information about the noun, the cat.

Underline the noun phrase in each sentence.

2 A tall man walked up the street.

3 The girl is wearing a red dress.

4 The sheep watched the bouncing lamb.

5 The hungry caterpillar is eating the plant.

Grammar 1

KEY SKILL

Pronouns are words you often use in place of a noun.
Here are some examples of pronouns:

I you he she it we they him her

The <u>dog</u> is eating.   **It** is eating.

TOP TIP!

More than one pronoun can be used in a sentence, for example,
'**He** can see that **they** are trying to catch **it**.'

WORKED EXAMPLE

Circle the pronoun in this sentence.

Ali passed (him) the ball.

The pronoun is 'him' because it replaces the name of the person (the noun) Ali passed the ball to.

Circle the pronoun or pronouns in each sentence.

6 We saw her at the shops.

7 Where are they going?

8 They are going to the playground.

9 The scarf looked like hers.

10 Can you see it?

KEY SKILL

To make sentences more interesting, **conjunctions** can be used to join smaller sentences together.

Conjunctions are **joining words**:   and   but   because   or   that

I always look forward to the summer.   The weather is usually sunny and warm.

I always look forward to the summer **because** the weather is usually sunny and warm.

WORKED EXAMPLE

Write a conjunction to finish these sentences.

Finn felt very tired after training .... he enjoyed it.

Finn felt very tired after training **but** he enjoyed it.

The conjunction 'but' joins the two sentences: 'Finn felt very tired after training.' and 'He enjoyed it.'

Write a conjunction to finish these sentences.

11   We went to the cinema .... Ellie came too.

12   I tidied my bedroom .... Mum said she would not let me out to play if I did not!

13   Shall I have ice cream .... shall I have chocolate?

14   I have a cold .... I still want to go swimming.

TOP TIP!

After adding the conjunction, always read the sentence to check it makes sense.

Total
21

6 Understanding Words

KEY SKILL

Understanding the meaning of words is important for knowing how to use them in the best way. If you do not understand the meaning of a word, always ask.

- **beautiful** means someone or something that is nice to look at

TOP TIP!

A dictionary gives you the meaning of words. The words are listed in alphabetical order.

Some words mean the same or are very similar in meaning. They are called **synonyms**.

- **small**   tiny   little   mini

WORKED EXAMPLE

Solve the clue using a **wh** or **ph** word from the box.

| elephant | dolphin | alphabet | wheel | white |

I am grey and I live in water.
dolphin

Read through all the words in the box before choosing the one that matches the meaning of the word. Both an elephant and a dolphin are grey but only the dolphin lives in water.

Solve the clues using a **wh** or **ph** word from the box.

| elephant | dolphin | alphabet | wheel | white |

1 I can help things move from one place to another. ....

2 I am very big and usually live in hot places. ....

3 I am a colour. ....

4 I am used to write words. ....

WORKED EXAMPLE

In this sentence, write what you think the word in **bold** means.

The girl hid **behind** the tree.

behind means <u>on the other side of</u>

In this sentence, **behind** explains that the girl is on the other side of the tree.

In each sentence, write what you think the word in **bold** means.

5 Amari wanted to **improve** his swimming.

improve means ....

6 Etta had a **great** birthday.

great means ....

WORKED EXAMPLE

Write a synonym for this word.

    horrible   bad

A similar meaning to the word **horrible** is **bad** but there are other words that also have similar meanings, like **awful** and **terrible**.

Write a synonym for each word.

7 quick ....   **8** tiny ....

9 shout ....   **10** cold ....

11 big ....   **12** chew ....

Total 12

7 Making Words

KEY SKILL

Some words are made from two shorter words that are put together. These are called **compound words**.

foot + ball = **football**

Sometimes a picture can give a clue to a word.

= **grass**

Some words have letters which are **silent**. When the word is said out loud, the silent letters are not said.

The word **write** is spoken **rite**.   The **w** is silent.

Some sounds in words are similar. It can be tricky to know what the correct spelling is, for example the **le**, **el**, **al** and **il** endings all sound similar.

padd<u>le</u>   jew<u>el</u>   pet<u>al</u>   foss<u>il</u>

WORKED EXAMPLE

Do the word sum. Write the compound words.

tooth + brush = **toothbrush**

If the word **tooth** and **brush** are joined they become the word **toothbrush**.

TOP TIP!

No changes are made to the smaller words when compound words are made.

Do the word sums. Write the compound words.

1 basket   +   ball   = ...

2 lunch   +   time   = ...

3 sand   +   castle = ...

4 snow   +   ball   = ...

WORKED EXAMPLE

This word has an unusual **o** sound.
Write a word to match the picture.

The picture shows a **glove**. The first letter is given to help you recognise the word.

g**love**

Each of these words has an unusual **o** sound.
Write a word to match each picture.

5

6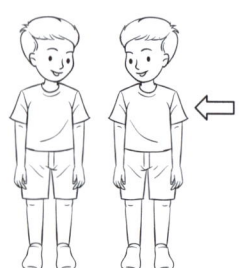

m ....   br ....

7 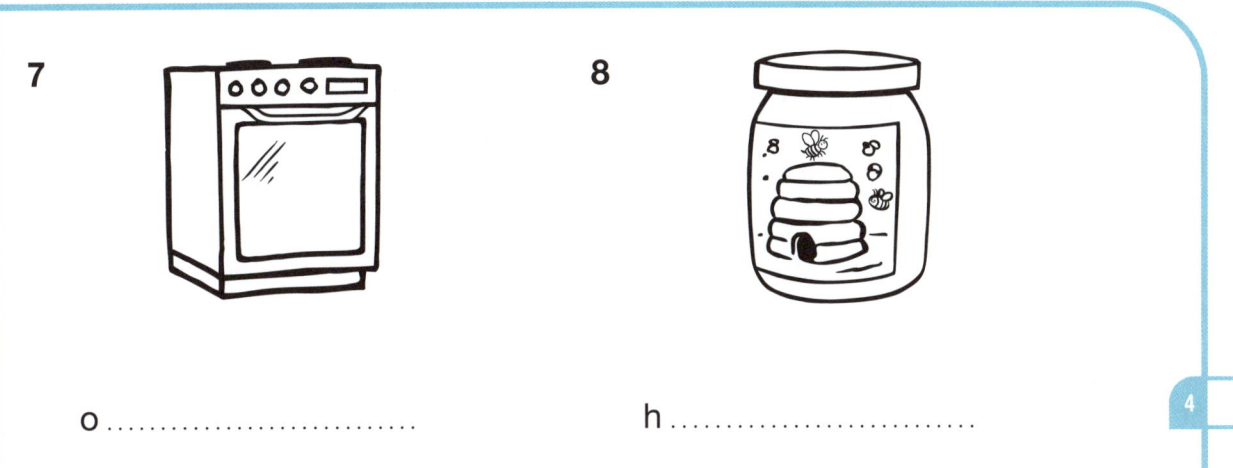 8

o .... h ....

WORKED EXAMPLE

Add the missing silent letters **k**, **g** or **w** to make a word.

 **w**rap

Say the word out loud. Add the missing silent letters **k**, **g** or **w** to make a word. There is a silent **w** in the word **wrap**.

Add the missing silent letters **k**, **g** or **w** to make a word.

9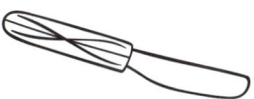

____nife

10 4 + 2 = 7 ✗

____rong

11

____nome

12

____nee

WORKED EXAMPLE

Add **le**, **el**, **al** or **il** to these words.

Then choose a word from the box with the same ending.

| nostril | middle | gravel | angle | petal |

padd**le**   **middle**

Add **le**, **el**, **al** or **il** to these words.

Then choose a word from the box with the same ending.

| nostril | middle | gravel | angle | petal |

13 rectang............ ....

14 ped............ ....

15 penc............ ....

16 trav............ ....

8 Grammar 2

> **KEY SKILL**
>
> A verb is a **doing** or **being** word.
> How a verb is written in a sentence tells us when the action happened.
>
> Remember, if an action is **happening now** it is written in the present tense.
>
> If an action has **already happened** it is written in the past tense.
>
> | | |
> |---|---|
> | When writing in the present tense we can use the verb. | I walk quickly. |
> | Another way is using a helper verb and adding the suffix **ing**. | I **am** walk**ing** quickly. |
> | When writing in the past tense we usually add the suffix **ed**. | I walk**ed** quickly. |
> | Another way is using a helper verb and adding the suffix **ing**. | I **was** walk**ing** quickly. |

WORKED EXAMPLE

Underline the two words that make the verb in these present tense sentences. The helper verb is **is** and the verb **to walk** has the suffix **ing** added.

The boy is walking.   The boy <u>is walking</u>.

Underline the two words that make the verb in these present tense sentences.

1 The cats are fighting.

2 Jake is bending his ruler.

3 The boys are throwing the ball.

4 Aimee is helping her dad.

5 Abdul is riding his bike.

6 The teachers are laughing.

WORKED EXAMPLE

Add the missing word to the table.

present tense (happening now)	past tense (happened in the past)
help	**helped**

The suffix **ed** is added to the verb to change it into the past tense. This is because the root word ends with two consonants and the suffix is added onto the end.

TOP TIP!

Remember the spelling rules when suffixes are added that begin with a vowel to root words. Look back at page 17 if you need to remind yourself.

7 Add the missing words to the table.

present tense (happening now)	past tense (happened in the past)
drum	
like	
prowl	
grab	

WORKED EXAMPLE

Add a verb to this sentence.

David .... towards the swings.   David **runs** towards the swings.

Many different verbs can be used to complete this sentence. The verb tells us how David moves towards the swings.

Add a different verb to each of these sentences.

8 Ilesh .... in the muddy puddle.

9 Fiona always .... her dog in the morning.

10 The children .... to be first in the pool.

11 The snowman .... in the sun.

12 Max quietly .... with Arjun.

KEY SKILL

An **adverb** tells us:

How something is done.   The boy talks **quietly**.

When something is done.   I walked to my nan's house **yesterday**.

Where something is done.   I left my ball **outside**.

WORKED EXAMPLE

Underline the adverb in this sentence. Write which type of adverb it is (how, when or where).

Tomorrow Kyle is going to a party.

<u>Tomorrow</u> Kyle is going to a party.   **when**

Tomorrow is the adverb that tells us **when** Kyle is going to the party.

Underline the adverb in these sentences.

Write which type of adverb it is (how, when or where).

13 The cat quickly jumped over the fence.   ....

14 Tuhil put his books over there.   ....

15 Laila never forgets her homework.   ....

16 I am going to wait inside.   ....

17 My mum wrote her name neatly.   ....

9 Choosing Words

> **KEY SKILL**
>
> Some words sound the same but are spelt differently and have different meanings. These words are called **homophones**.
>
> **Wear** and **where** sound the same but mean different things.
>
> I will <u>wear</u> my hat today.   <u>Where</u> is my hat?

WORKED EXAMPLE

Underline the homophone for the word in bold.

hole   hollow   <u>whole</u>   who

In this homophone there is a silent letter. The word **whole** begins with a silent **w** so it sounds the same as **hole**. This makes it a homophone of the word **hole**.

Underline a homophone for each of the words in bold.

1 **brake**   broke   bring   break

2 **hare**   here   hair   hurry

3 **blue**   black   blow   blew

4 **four**   focus   for   found

KEY SKILL

There are many words that have the same vowel sound, but that sound is spelled differently.

Watch out for these sounds.

a-e	flame	ai	snail	ay	play
ee	sweet	ea	stream	e-e	these
i-e	slide	igh	high	y	why
o-e	smoke	oa	boat	ow	window
u-e	cube	oo	moon	ew	screw

TOP TIP!

When writing rhyming words watch out for letter patterns that are the same.

WORKED EXAMPLE

Add a word to each column of the table.

igh words	i-e words	y words
tight	smile	spy

Each of these words have the same sound, even though the sound in these words is spelled differently.

Add a word to each column of the table.

5

igh words	i-e words	y words

KEY SKILL

Always watch out for words that are spelled incorrectly.

To check if a word is spelled correctly:

- try writing it a few different ways and see which way looks right.
- use a dictionary and look up the word.

WORKED EXAMPLE

Circle the correct spelling of this word.

wosh   (wash)

The **wa** lettering makes the correct sound for the word **wash**. **Wosh** is not a word.

Circle the correct spelling of each of these words.

6   werk   work

7   squash   sqush

8   worm   wurm

9   wunder   wander

4

Total 14

Puzzle 1

KEY SKILL

The letter **c** can make two different sounds:

- hard c
- soft c

An example of a **hard c** is **cat**.   or   A **soft c** example is **circle** which sounds like **s**.

The letter **g** can also make two different sounds:

- hard g
- soft g

An example of a **hard g** is **gate**.   or   A **soft g** example is **giant** which sounds like **j**.

Find five **soft c** words hidden in the wordsearch. Write the words.

t	h	u	r	a	c	e	y
c	f	m	i	y	s	c	o
e	q	o	c	o	s	a	p
m	u	n	e	a	y	t	n
e	o	d	y	w	w	o	d
n	b	i	c	y	c	l	e
t	r	y	u	c	o	l	d

....

....

....

....

....

Find five **soft g** words hidden in the wordsearch. Write the words.

t	m	y	l	e	p	d	s
b	r	i	d	g	e	a	h
g	o	l	d	g	k	j	u
o	g	b	r	s	r	m	g
o	g	i	r	a	f	f	e
d	y	q	n	g	a	m	e
e	m	t	k	e	g	o	p

....

....

....

....

....

Total 10

42

Mixed Papers

Mixed Paper 1

Comprehension

My Eyes are Watering

I've got a cold
And that is why
My eyes are watering.

It's nothing to do
With getting caught
When I planned
To SMASH
The rounders ball
SO FAR
That it would go
Into PERMANENT ORBIT
Round the school.

It would've done, too –
If Lucy Smith
Hadn't RUSHED
To catch it.

'Look at Trevor –
He's having a cry!'
Not true.
I've got a cold
And THAT is why
My eyes are watering.

OK?

By *Trevor Harvey*

Underline the right answers.

1. What game was Trevor playing?

    a football   **b** rounders   **c** netball

2. How did Trevor plan to hit the ball?

    a a smash high in the air   **b** a smash along the ground

    c a smash behind him

Answer these questions.

3. Copy a line from the poem that shows Trevor was going to hit the ball hard.

    ....

4. Do you think Trevor really had a cold? Why?

    ....

    ....

The alphabet

Write the word for each picture. Then write two more words that start with the same letter.

5.

    ....

    ....

    ....

6.

    ....

    ....

    ....

Grammar

Underline the nouns and circle the adjectives.

7   nose   grey   swarm

   spiky   London   wooden

Underline the verb in each sentence.

8 Moad jumped off the wall.

9 We quickly ran up the road.

10 Iona sat on the comfortable chair.

11 They swam across the river.

Spelling

Add a suffix to each word to make a new word.

12 pain.................................

13 enjoy.................................

14 sad.................................

15 hope.................................

Choosing words

Choose two more words to add to each column of the table. All the words need to have the same **oa**, **ow**, **o-e** sound.

16

oa words	ow words	o-e words
boat	low	spoke

TOP TIP!

Be careful. The 'ow' letter pattern can have other sounds.

Sentences

Write a question that each statement answers.

17 Statement: Brian went swimming at 3 o'clock.

Question: ....

18 Statement: Ajin went to Mark's house for tea.

Question: ....

19 Statement: The school fair is on the 16th May.

Question: ....

Understanding words

Solve the clues using words ending in **y** or **ey** from the box.

| valley | money | spy |

20 A person looking for secret information.   ....

21 An area of land set between hills.   ....

22 Needed to pay for things.   ....

Punctuation

Copy the sentences and add the missing capital letters and punctuation.

23 at school i work very hard

....

24 watch out for the bus

....

25 meena says i am her best friend

....

26 do you live in birmingham

....

> **TOP TIP!**
> Think carefully about the capital letters that are needed. Most of the sentences need two!

Making words

Add the missing silent letters **k** or **w** to make a word.

27

___nit

28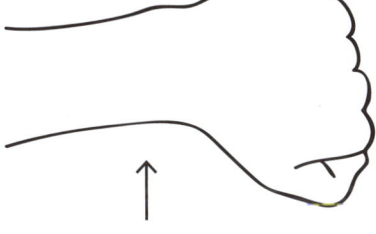

___rist

29

___ not

30

___ restle

Mixed Paper 2

Comprehension

Your pet rabbit

Rabbits are usually friendly animals. You can get big rabbits and small ones called dwarf rabbits. Some have ears that stand up straight and others have lop ears. They are easy pets to keep but must be kept clean and always have food and water available.

Looking after your rabbit

Every day your pet rabbit needs to be given fresh dried food and fresh water. They enjoy nibbling hay which can be bought from your local pet shop. If your rabbit lives in a hutch and does not have a run it is important to give it some greens from the garden. Rabbits particularly enjoy dandelion leaves. Rabbits need their hutches to be cleaned out regularly. They need clean sawdust or straw. No animal likes sleeping in a dirty bed.

Watch out!

The claws and teeth of rabbits can sometimes grow too long. If this ever happens, take your rabbit to the vet and they will trim them for you. If you do not it could be very painful for your rabbit.

Always be careful as some rabbits are very clever at escaping and if they get out of their hutch they can run very fast!

Underline the right answers.

1 What two things must rabbits always have available?

   a food   **b** a plastic dish

   c water   **d** a brush

2 Where should you take your rabbit if its claws grow too long?

   a the garden   **b** a pet shop

   c the vet   **d** for a walk

Answer these questions.

3 What do rabbits particularly enjoy eating?

   ....

4 Why is it important to clean out your rabbit's cage regularly?

   ....

5 If you were a rabbit what would you least like about being a pet?

   ....

Choosing words

With a line, link the homophones.

6 knew   flour   right   here   ate

   hear   write   flower   eight   new

> **TOP TIP!**
>
> Saying the words out loud makes it easier to link the homophones because they sound the same!

Punctuation

Copy these sentences and add the missing **apostrophes**.

7 Weve collected the balls.

....

8 Ill be back soon.

....

9 Whats the time?

....

The alphabet

There are three letters missing in this **alphabet**. Which letters are they?

a b c e f g h i j k l m o p r s t u v w x y z

10 _____   **11** _____   **12** _____

TOP TIP!

Saying the alphabet out loud will help make the missing letters clear.

Understanding words

Write a word with a similar meaning for each word.

13 hot ....   **14** yell ....

15 quick ....   **16** nice ....

Spelling

Circle the word that is spelled correctly.

17	beging	begging	18	jokeer	joker
19	flatest	flattest	20	runny	runy
21	fitter	fiter	22	waveing	waving

Sentences

Read these sentences. Write whether they happened in the **past** or are happening in the **present**.

23 Max is eating an ice cream. ....

24 Ola jumped into the swimming pool. ....

25 I am reading a great book. ....

26 Cian cheered as his friend won the race. ....

Grammar

Add a conjunction from the box to each sentence. Use each word only once.

| and | but | because | that |

27 Adam continued to work .... he felt very tired.

28 Salima dried her hair .... it got wet in the rain.

29 Lee washed the dishes .... were next to the sink.

30 Janu ate her breakfast .... she left for school.

Circle the pronouns in these sentences.

31 I went to the shop.

32 They ate bananas.

33 Can we go swimming?

Making words

Each of these words has a **soft c**.
Write a word to match each picture.

34

f..............................

35

s..............................

36

p..............................

37

d..............................

Mixed Paper 3

Comprehension

Hippo was strong. He was very strong.
He was stronger than all the other animals.

"I am stronger than all of you," said Hippo. "Therefore, I am going to be your king and leader."

The other animals scowled. They didn't want Hippo as their king and leader; he was stubborn and bad-tempered.

"I want to be king," said Monkey. "I'm strong, too. I'll show you. I'll pull you out of that lake."

"Bah!" snorted Hippo. "Why don't you try? If you pull me out of this lake, you can be king. If I pull you into the lake, then you will have to go away and find somewhere else to live."

Monkey went to find a strong rope.

"Hold this end," he said to Hippo, "but don't start pulling until I tell you."

Monkey disappeared among a clump of trees and tied the other end of the rope to the biggest tree he could find. "Pull!" he shouted.

Hippo pulled ... and pulled ... and pulled. He pulled until his face was red and he was out of breath. He pulled again, but still he didn't pull Monkey into the lake.

"Monkey is strong," he said, gloomily, and waded out of the lake. At that moment, Monkey popped out from behind a tree ...

Hippo and Monkey, a Nigerian folk tale

Underline the right answers.

1 Which animal was the strongest?

   a Monkey   **b** Hippo   **c** another animal

2 When Hippo was pulling the rope, could he see Monkey?

   a yes   **b** no   **c** sometimes

Answer these questions.

3 Write a description of what Hippo was like.

....

....

4 What do you think Monkey said to Hippo when he ran out of the trees?

....

....

The alphabet

5–8

Put these words in alphabetical order.

| rubber | pencil | sharpener | crayon |

(1) .... (2) ....

(3) .... (4) ....

Understanding words

In each sentence, write what you think the word in **bold** means.

9

The post woman was **startled** by the barking.

startled means ....

10

Kim **soaked** her brother with water.

soaked means ....

Choosing words

Circle the correct spelling of each of these words.

11 people   peple   peeple

12 evrybody   everybody   evurybody

13 childrn   childdren   children

14 climb   clim   climbe

Punctuation

Write each of these using an **apostrophe**.

15 the flute belonging to Nazar ....

16 the food belonging to the goat ....

17 the bag belonging to the teacher ....

18 the bark belonging to the dog ....

19 the bike belonging to Sam ....

Spelling

Write the plural of each of these words.

20 fox ....   21 spy ....

22 blotch ....   23 copy ....

24 chimney ....   25 candle ....

Grammar

Circle a verb and underline a noun phrase in each sentence.

26   The muddy dog swam in the river.

27   We ate some sticky sweets.

28   They jumped onto the brick wall.

29   The black cat sleeps by the fire.

30   We go to the best school in the area.

Change each adjective into a **how** adverb by adding **ly**. Write each adverb into a sentence.

Example: loud............   loud**ly**   Freya spoke loudly.

31   quick......................   ....

32   brave......................   ....

33   proud......................   ....

34   close......................   ....

Sentences

Rearrange the words so the sentence makes sense.

35 my for tomorrow. birthday party wait I cannot

....

36 today? Who you to visit would like

....

Mixed Paper 4

Comprehension

Slick Nick's Dog's Tricks

Slick Nick's dog does tricks.

The tricks Nick's dog does are slick.

He picks up sticks, stands on bricks,
⁵ Nick's finger clicks, the dog barks SIX! He picks a mix of doggy bix then gives Slick Nick thick sloppy licks. Mick and Rick's dog's not so quick – kicks the bricks, drops the sticks, can't bark to
¹⁰ six, is in a fix, gets Mick and Rick to do its tricks, gets on their wicks despite its mix of waggy tail and loving licks – but Slick Nick's dog does tricks. The tricks Nick's dog does are slick.

By *David Harmer*

Underline the right answer.

1   How many times does Nick's dog bark?

   a four   **b** five   **c** six

2   What does Mick and Rick's dog do with sticks?

   a catches sticks   **b** drops sticks   **c** picks up sticks

Answer these questions.

3 Who does Mick and Rick's dog get to do his tricks?

....

4 Nick's dog gives him **sloppy licks** (line 6). Write another word for **sloppy**.

....

Spelling

Add the prefix **dis** or **un** to each word to make a word with the opposite meaning.

5 ....do   **6** ....fortunate

7 ....obeyed   **8** ....kind

9 ....sure   **10** ....like

Sentences

Write two sentences. One that happened in the **past** and one that is happening in the **present**.

Example: past   I walked to school.

                 present   I am eating my breakfast.

11 past ....

12 present ....

> **TOP TIP!**
> Think about something that is happening now and something that happened yesterday.

Choosing words

Underline a homophone for each of the words in blue.

13	**wear**	were	wore	where
14	**hole**	pole	whole	hall
15	**no**	now	knot	know
16	**sure**	shore	shell	pure

Punctuation

Finish the sentence below with the things on the list. Do not forget the commas.

> *Things to remember:*
>
> **towel   brush   drink   goggles**
>
> **swimming costume**

17 When we went swimming we had to remember a ....

....

....

Write the two words as one word. Do not forget the apostrophe!

18 must not ....

19 have not ....

20 was not ....

21 should not ....

The alphabet

There are three letters missing in each alphabet. Which letters are they?

a b c d f g h i j k m n o p q r s t u v x y z

22 ____   **23** ____   **24** ____

a b c d e f g h k l m n o p q s t u v w x y z

25 ____   **26** ____   **27** ____

Grammar

Underline the adjective in each sentence.

28 Tuhil has the longest legs.

29 Gemma is the youngest at the party.

30 Dan's story is shorter than Mia's.

Finish these sentences by adding the helper verb. Fill the gaps correctly with **is** or **are**.

31 Ten children .... playing on the climbing frame.

32 Lucy .... going to Arwa's house for tea.

33 Adele and Harvey .... going on holiday.

Making words

Do the word sums. Write the compound words.

34 bed + room = ...

35 hair + cut = ...

36 sun + flower = ...

37 eye + brow = ...

Understanding words

Write a word that has a similar meaning.

38 fast .... **39** leap ....

40 sad .... **41** ill ....

42 scream .... **43** tired ....

Mixed Paper 5

Comprehension

The Life Cycle of a Frog

A frog lays some eggs.

The egg is protected by a jelly-like material.

The tail-bud begins to grow.

The tadpole wriggles free and attaches to some weed.

The back legs begin to grow.

Then front legs grow.

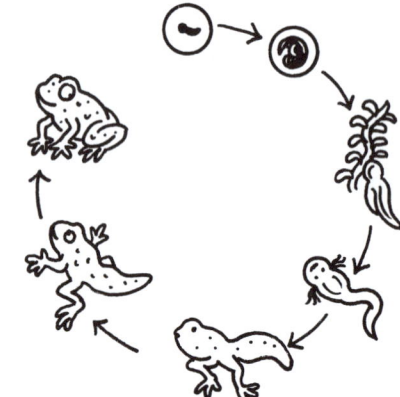

After about eleven weeks the frog is fully grown and can leave the water.

Underline the right answers.

1 What is the egg protected by?

    a a jelly-like material   **b** pond weed   **c** the frog

2 Which legs grow first?

    a the front legs   **b** the back legs   **c** both together

Answer these questions.

3 About how many weeks does it take an egg to grow into a frog?

    ....

4 Why do you think the tadpole attaches to some weed when it leaves the jelly-like material?

....

....

The alphabet

a b c d e f g h i j k l m n o p q r s t u v w x y z

Write a word that starts with the 5th letter of the alphabet.
Example: elephant

5 Write a word that starts with the 7th letter of the alphabet. ....

6 Write a word that starts with the 11th letter of the alphabet. ....

7 Write a word that starts with the 16th letter of the alphabet. ....

8 Write a word that starts with the 22nd letter of the alphabet. ....

Sentences

Use the picture to make up different types of sentences which link to the picture.

9   statement   ....

10 question   ....

11 exclamation ....

12 command   ....

Understanding words

Solve the clues using a word with **wa** in it.

13 I am a large white bird often found on rivers. ....

14 I tell the time and go on your wrist. ....

15 I do this to my hands when they are dirty. ....

Spelling

Add the missing words to the table.

16

	+ er	+ est
smoky	**smokier**	**smokiest**
cloudy		
creaky		
smelly		

Punctuation

Copy each sentence and add the missing apostrophes.

17 Mias brother went shopping but didnt like it.

....

18 It hasnt been this cold for a long time.

....

19 Jacobs coat fell on the floor.

....

Choosing words

Write two words ending in **al** and two words ending in **il**.

20 al ....

21 il ....

Circle the words with a **soft c**, like **c** in face.

22   cry   city   copy   catch   centre   ice

Grammar

Underline the adverb in these sentences.

Write which type of adverb it is (how, when or where).

23 I left my game downstairs. ....

24 Yesterday we went to see the circus. ....

25 We slowly walked home after school. ....

Circle the pronoun or pronouns in each sentence.

26 He looked at me with surprise.

27 When can I come home?

28 They are mine.

29 She really liked his story.

Making words

Add the missing vowel letter to finish each word. The clues will help.

30   m __ ny   (lots of)

31   gr __ at   (very good)

32   w __ ter   (a liquid)

33   aft __ r   (opposite of 'before')

Mixed Paper 6

Comprehension

George had just started school. At the beginning of the week he was in the reception class, by the end he was in Year 6. George was a very talented child, in
5 fact he was top of the top class. At the end of his first week at school he went to bed saying he felt tired … suddenly there was an awful wailing coming from his bedroom.

"I'm coming, my baby!" called George's
10 mother. "Mummy's coming!" and she rushed upstairs to find George sitting up in bed, sobbing his heart out. This was not the confident self-assured know-it-all cleverest child in the school. This was just a frightened baby, and she cuddled him as fiercely as she had when he was only tiny and had never spoken a word. "What is it, George
15 darling?" she said as she mopped away his tears. "Did you have a bad dream?"

"I did, I did, Mummy!" sobbed George.

"What is it? Tell Mummy."

Gradually George's sobs turned to sniffles, and then he blew his nose
20 and said, "I dreamt we were doing a science test at school."

"A science test?"

"Yes, we do science in the new curriculum, you know. And there was a simple question in it that I couldn't answer, and I cried like a baby. I cried in the dream, and I was crying when I woke up. I really must
25 apologise for behaving so childishly."

"Poor lamb!" said his mother. "What was the question?"

"It was the order of events in the cycle of the internal combustion engine," said George.

"Forget about it, George," said his mother sadly. "I expect that there'll be lots of questions you won't know the answers to."

"Not if I can help it," said George.

"Anyway, don't worry. Just go back to sleep. Mummy's here."

"Oh, I shan't worry any more, Mother," said George in his usual confident tones. "I've remembered it now. It's Induction – Compression – Ignition – Exhaust," and exhausted, he lay back and went happily to sleep.

From *George Starts School* by *Dick King-Smith*

Underline the right answers.

1 What test did George dream about?

   a a maths test   b a spelling test   c a science test

2 Why did George apologise to his mother?

   a for not knowing the answer   b for waking up

   c for behaving childishly

Answer these questions.

3 Write two words that could be used to describe George.

   ....

4 Write two reasons why you think George was exhausted when "he lay back and went happily to sleep" (line 36).

   (1) ....

   (2) ....

Choosing words

Circle the word spelled incorrectly.

5 children   televishun   half   sugar

6 muther   break   improve   money

7 should   brother   plant   meny

8 steak   tresure   beautiful   grass

Spelling

9 Write two words with the prefix **un**. ....

10 Write two words with the prefix **dis**. ....

Punctuation

Write these sentences correctly.

11 this morning clare asked if she could come to my house

    ....

12 shall i bring my pillow sleeping bag and tent

    ....

13 on monday i am going on holiday

    ....

Making words

Add the missing letter to spell each word correctly. Use the clues to help.

g r **e** a t   Clue: really good

14   b e a ___ t i f u l   Clue: very pretty

15   f ___ t h e r   Clue: a dad

16   b e ___ i n d   Clue: opposite of in front

17   i m ___ r o v e   Clue: to get better

Write four words that include a **soft g**.

18   ....

   ....

Grammar

Finish these sentences by adding the helper verb. Fill the gaps correctly with **was** or **were**.

19   The dog .... walking on the lead.

20   The children .... riding the ponies.

21   Leena .... cooking a cake.

22   We .... going to go to the zoo but it is raining.

Finish the sentences. Each sentence must use the conjunction (joining word) in the box.

23 | but | When ....

....

24 | or | What ....

....

25 | so | Shall ....

....

The alphabet

Write these words in alphabetical order.

walk   swim   run   crawl

26 (1) ....   **27** (2) ....

28 (3) ....   **29** (4) ....

Understanding words

Sort the letters to find a word ending in **tion**. The clues will help.

Example: e t o i s n c   (a part)   **section**

30 t o s a t i n   (where trains stop)   ....

31 o i o t m n (movement) ....

32 n i t i f c o (stories) ....

33 r d t i i e o n c (an arrow shows this) ....

Sentences

Write these whole sentences in the correct order so they make sense.

Then he found the robe he lost last year.

Once upon a time a king lost his crown.

In the end he found his crown, it was in the bathroom!

While he was searching, he found his glasses.

34 (1) ....

....

35 (2) ....

....

36 (3) ....

....

37 (4) ....

....

Total 45

Puzzle 2

Look carefully at this index page. Can you answer the questions?

1 On which page of the book would you find out about medicine?

....

2 What two subjects can you find out about on page 27?

....

Index

accidents	12, 27	grooming	8
ailments	3–5		
		health	3, 22
bathing	28	hygiene	23
beds	14, 16		
bones	27	injuries	29–30
breed types	35–36		
		kennels	14
claws	6		
collars	2	leads	3
Dalmatians	35	mating	34
		medicine	5
ears	4, 12, 24		
exercise	2–3	nits	4
eyes	25		
		paws	2, 10
feeding	7	puppies	35
first aid	10		
fleas	5		

3 This index is for a book. What do you think the book is about?

....

4 Which letters of the alphabet before 'p' do not have an entry in this index?

....

Total 4

76

Keywords

Some special words are used in this book. You will find them in **bold** the first time they appear in the Papers. These words are explained here.

adjective	a word that describes somebody or something, for example 'tall'
adverb	a word that describes how, when or where something is done, for example 'quickly', 'yesterday', 'behind'
alphabetical order	words arranged in the order found in the alphabet
collective noun	the names of groups of things, for example 'swarm'
command	a sentence that tells someone to do something
common noun	the names of ordinary things, for example 'house'
compound word	a word made up of two other words, for example 'football'
conjunction	a word that joins sentences, phrases or words, for example 'and', 'because'
consonant letters	all letters of the alphabet apart from a, e, i, o, u (vowel letters)
contraction	joining two words together by leaving out some letters and adding an apostrophe, for example 'do not = don't'
exclamation	a sentence which expresses strong feeling
homophone	words that sound the same but have different meanings and/or spellings, for example 'two' and 'to'
noun	a word that names a person, place, thing or idea, for example 'book'
noun phrase	a phrase about a noun, for example 'the tall man'
past tense	something that has already happened
phrase	a group of words that stand together as a unit in a sentence

Keywords

plural	more than one, for example 'cats'
prefix	a group of letters put at the beginning of a word, for example 'un', 'dis'
present tense	something happening now
pronoun	a word often put in place of a noun, for example 'she', 'he'
proper noun	the name of a person, place, a day and month, for example 'Ben'
question	a sentence that asks something
statement	a sentence which gives information
suffix	a group of letters put at the end of a word *ly, ing*
syllable	A part of a word that contains sounds of a word
synonym	a word with a very similar meaning to another word, for example 'quick' and 'fast'
verb	a 'doing' or 'being' word
vowel letters	the letters a, e, i, o, u

Notes

Notes

Answers

Answers will vary for questions that require children to answer in their own words. Possible answers to most of these questions are given in *italics*.

Learning Paper 1: Comprehension and the Alphabet (pages 6–11)

1. **a** Instruction one says, "Draw a simple shape on a piece of thin sponge …"
2. **c** Instruction three says, "When the paint on the sponge runs out, you can add more to continue printing."
3. **a** Instruction two says, "Cut out your shape carefully …" but in the list of things needed there is nothing to cut the shape out with.
4. The following are examples of verbs found in the instructions: *draw, cut, cover, stick, press, add.*
5. *If you do not wait for the glue to dry, the sponge will come away from the cardboard when you try and print.*
6. Some examples of what the printed paper might be used for are: *wrapping paper, covering a book, framing a picture.*
7. **c**
8. **k**
9. **t**
10. **i**
11. **p**
12. **v**
13. **car** Two words that begin with the letter 'c', for example: *cake, carpet, cot, copy, cloud.*
14. **tree** Two words that begin with the letter 't', for example: *tiger, toast, toad, twig, tray.*
15. **ear**
16. **head**
17. **mouth**
18. **nose**

Learning Paper 2: Punctuation (pages 12–15)

1–3 Each sentence starts with a capital letter.
1. **We are going on holiday.** This statement finishes with a full stop.
2. **Quick, take over!** This exclamation finishes with an exclamation mark.
3. **Did the dog get the ball?** This question finishes with a question mark.
4–6 Commas are used to separate items in a list.
4. **Elena loves maths, history, sport, art and science.**
5. **Ronan bought bread, milk, crisps, cream and sweets at the shop.**
6. **On holiday we travelled by boat, car, bus, train and plane.**
7. **I'll** The apostrophe replaces the letters 'wi'.
8. **they're** The apostrophe replaces the letter 'a'.
9. **he's** The apostrophe replaces the letter 'i'.
10. **we've** The apostrophe replaces the letters 'ha'.
11–13 The apostrophe is used to indicate possession.
11. **Zola's pillow**
12. **the farmer's tractor**
13. **Amar's scream**

Learning Paper 3: Spelling (pages 16–19)

1. **foxes** Fox ends in 'x' so 'es' is added to make it plural.
2. **bushes** Bush ends in 'sh' so 'es' is added to make it plural.
3. **trains** Just an 's' is added to make 'train' plural.
4. **babies** Baby ends in a consonant and 'y' so the 'y' is changed to an 'i' and 'es' is added to make it plural.
5. **monkeys** Monkey ends in a vowel and a 'y' so an 's' is added to make it plural.
6. **churches** Church ends in 'ch' so 'es' is added to make it plural.

Learning Papers 3–6

7–8 These words have one syllable and end with a vowel and a consonant so the consonant is doubled before adding the suffix.
  7 **batter**
  8 **saddest**

9–10 These words end with a consonant and 'e' so the 'e' is dropped before adding the suffix.
  9 **nicest**
  10 **shiny**

11–12 These words end in a consonant and 'y', so the 'y' is changed to an 'i' before the suffix is added.
  11 **cried**
  12 **copier**

13–18 These suffixes each begin with a consonant so no changes are needed when they are added to these words.
  13 **agreement**
  14 **painful**
  15 **fearless**
  16 **sadness**
  17 **treatment**
  18 **quickly**

19–24 When 'un' or 'dis' are added to a word it changes the word to its opposite meaning.
  19 **untie**
  20 **disagree**
  21 **disappear**
  22 **distrust**
  23 **untrue**
  24 **untidy**

Learning Paper 4: Sentences
(pages 20–23)

1 **Where have all the sweets gone?**
2 **Sit down on the benches at the back of the room** or **Sit down at the back of the room on the benches.**

3–5 The questions must all start with a capital letter and end with a question mark.
  3 *How old is Kisha?*
  4 *Where did Tim go after school?*
  5 *How did Liam get to Tayah's house?*

6–9 The following are examples of a statement, question, exclamation and command.
  6 *The giraffe is taller than the dog.*
  7 *Does the giraffe like the dog?*
  8 *Wow, the giraffe is tall!*
  9 *Measure how tall the giraffe is.*
  10 **past** It has already happened.
  11 **present** It is happening now.
  12 **past** It has already happened.
  13 **present** It is happening now.
  14 **present** It is happening now.

Learning Paper 5: Grammar 1
(pages 24–27)

1 Underlined: **sausage, kite, herd, America, June** Circled: **dirty, long, soft**

2–5 A noun phrase is a phrase that gives more information about the noun.
  2 <u>A tall man</u> walked up the street.
  3 The girl is wearing <u>a red dress</u>.
  4 The sheep watched <u>the bouncing lamb</u>.
  5 <u>The hungry caterpillar</u> is eating the plant.

6–10 Pronouns are words often used to replace a noun.
  6 **We** saw **her** at the shops.
  7 Where are **they** going?
  8 **They** are going to the playground.
  9 The scarf looked like **hers**.
  10 Can **you** see it?

11–14 A conjunction is a joining word. Here the conjunction joins two sentences.
  11 *and*
  12 *because*
  13 *or*
  14 *but*

Learning Paper 6: Understanding Words
(pages 28–30)

1 **wheel**
2 **elephant**
3 **white**
4 **alphabet**
5 *get better at*
6 *really good*

7–12 Synonyms are words with similar meanings.
  7 *fast*
  8 *small*
  9 *yell*
  10 *freezing*
  11 *large*
  12 *bite*

Learning Paper 7: Making Words
(pages 31–34)

1–4 Compound words are made when two smaller words are joined together.
1. **basketball**
2. **lunchtime**
3. **sandcastle**
4. **snowball**
5. **money**
6. **brother**
7. **oven**
8. **honey**

9–12 Silent letters are letters that cannot be heard in a word.
9. **k**nife
10. **w**rong
11. **g**nome
12. **k**nee

13–16 The spelling of words with 'le', 'el', 'il' and 'al' can be tricky as they sound very similar.
13. rectang**le**   ang**le**
14. ped**al**   pet**al**
15. penc**il**   nostr**il**
16. trav**el**   grav**el**

Learning Paper 8: Grammar 2
(pages 35–38)

1–6 Helper verbs sit alongside and support the verb.
1. The cats <u>are fighting</u>.
2. Jake <u>is bending</u> his ruler.
3. The boys <u>are throwing</u> the ball.
4. Aimee <u>is helping</u> her dad.
5. Abdul <u>is riding</u> his bike.
6. The teachers <u>are laughing</u>.
7.

present tense (happening now)	past tense (happened in the past)
drum	**drummed**
like	**liked**
prowl	**prowled**
grab	**grabbed**

8–12 A verb is a 'doing' or 'being' word.
8. *jumps*
9. *walks*
10. *rush*
11. *melts*
12. *talks*

13–17 An adverb tells us how, when or where something is done.
13. The cat <u>quickly</u> jumped over the fence.   **how**
14. Tuhil put his books over <u>there</u>.   **where**
15. Laila <u>never</u> forgets her homework.   **when**
16. I am going to wait <u>inside</u>.   **where**
17. My mum wrote her name <u>neatly</u>.   **how**

Learning Paper 9: Choosing Words
(pages 39–41)

1–4 A homophone is a word that sounds the same but is spelled differently and has a different meaning.
1. **break**
2. **hair**
3. **blew**
4. **for**
5. *light, fight, bright, pile, while, tile, sly, fly, sky*
6. **work**
7. **squash**
8. **worm**
9. **wander**

Puzzle 1 (pages 42)

Soft c words – **race, rice, bicycle, cement, ace**
Soft g words – **huge, gym, giraffe, bridge, ridge**

Mixed Paper 1 (pages 43–47)

1. **b**
2. **a**
3. One of the following:
'Into permanent orbit'
'To SMASH'
'SO FAR'.
4. An answer stating they do not think Trevor has a cold, he is upset and frustrated about Lucy catching the ball.
5. **horse** Two further words beginning with 'h', for example: *hug, hat*.
6. **paddle** Two further words beginning with 'p', for example: *pot, page*.

Mixed Papers 1–2

7 **nose, swarm, London** are nouns.
These are examples of a common noun, a collective noun and a proper noun. See keywords on pages 77–78 for their definitions.
grey, spiky, wooden are adjectives.
An adjective is a word used to describe somebody or something.

8–11 A verb is a 'doing' or 'being' word.
8 Moad <u>jumped</u> off the wall.
9 We quickly <u>ran</u> up the road.
10 Iona <u>sat</u> on the comfortable chair.
11 They <u>swam</u> across the river.

12–15 There are a few different suffixes that can be used. The following are examples:
12 *painful*
13 *enjoyment*
14 *sadness*
15 *hopeful*

16

oa words	ow words	o-e words
boat	low	spoke
coat	slow	poke
goat	blow	smoke

17–19 Each question must be answered by the statement.
17 *When did Brian go swimming?*
18 *Why did Ajin go to Mark's house?*
19 *When is the school fair?*
20 **spy**
21 **valley**
22 **money**

23–26 Capital letters are needed for the beginning of a sentence, proper nouns and the word 'I'. Punctuation is needed at the end of each of these sentences.
23 **A**t school **I** work very hard.
24 **W**atch out for the bus!
25 **M**eena says **I** am her best friend.
26 **D**o you live in **B**irmingham?
27 **k**nit
28 **w**rist
29 **k**not
30 **w**restle

Mixed Paper 2 (pages 48–52)

1 **a, c**
2 **c**
3 **dandelion leaves**
4 *No animal likes sleeping in a dirty bed.*
5 *For example, I would not like to kept in a cage, I would rather be free.*
6 Homophones are words that sound the same but are spelled differently and have different meanings.
flour – flower
right – write
here – hear
ate – eight

7–9 Apostrophes for contraction show where letters are missed out of a word.
7 We've collected the balls. (We've = we have)
8 I'll be back soon. (I'll = I will)
9 What's the time. (What's = what is)
10 **d**
11 **n**
12 **q**

13–16 There can be number of similar words to those listed.
13 *sizzling*
14 *scream*
15 *fast*
16 *lovely*

17–22 Understanding the correct spelling of these words suggests there is an understanding of adding suffixes to one syllable words that end in a vowel and consonant and those which end in 'e'.
17 **begging**
18 **joker**
19 **flattest**
20 **runny**
21 **fitter**
22 **waving**
23 **present**
24 **past**
25 **present**
26 **past**

27–30 Conjunctions are joining words.
27 Adam continued to work **but** he felt very tired.
28 Salima dried her hair **because** it got wet in the rain.
29 Lee washed the dishes **that** were next to the sink.
30 Janu ate her breakfast **and** she left for school.

31–33 A pronoun is a word used in place of a noun.

31 **I** went to the shop.
32 **They** ate bananas.
33 Can **we** go swimming?
34–37 A soft c sounds like an 's' in the word.
34 **face**
35 **space**
36 **price**
37 **dice**

Mixed Paper 3 (pages 53–58)

1 b
2 b
3 *Hippo was strong, stubborn and bad-tempered.*
4 An answer stating what they think Monkey said to Hippo, suggesting Monkey was pleased with himself, possibly laughing at Hippo and pointing out how clever he was.
5–8 Alphabetical order is the order the initial letters of the word are placed in the alphabet.
5 **crayon**
6 **pencil**
7 **rubber**
8 **sharpener**
9 *surprised*
10 *made very wet*
11 **people**
12 **everybody**
13 **children**
14 **climb**
15–18 Apostrophes for possession show when one thing belongs to another.
15 **Nazar's flute**
16 **the goat's food**
17 **the teacher's bag**
18 **the dog's bark**
19 **Sam's bike**
20–25 Just 's' is added to many words to make them plural however, if a word ends in 's', 'x', 'ch' or 'sh' an 'es' is added. If a word ends in 'y' change the 'y' to an 'i' before adding 'es', but if the letter before the 'y' is a vowel, just add 's'.
20 **foxes**
21 **spies**
22 **blotches**
23 **copies**
24 **chimneys**
25 **candles**
26–30 A verb is a 'doing' or 'being' word. A noun phrase is a group of words that gives more information about a noun.
26 <u>The muddy dog</u> **swam** in the river.
27 We **ate** <u>some sticky sweets.</u>
28 They **jumped** onto <u>the brick wall.</u>
29 <u>The black cat</u> **sleeps** by the fire.
30 We **go** to <u>the best school</u> in the area.
31–34 Each of the adverbs below need to be written into a sentence.
31 **quickly** (Students' own answers)
32 **bravely** (Students' own answers)
33 **proudly** (Students' own answers)
34 **closely** (Students' own answers)
35 **I cannot wait for my birthday party tomorrow.**
36 **Who would you like to visit today?**

Mixed Paper 4 (pages 59–63)

1 c
2 b
3 **Mick and Rick**
4 *wet*
5–10 A prefix is added to the beginning of a word to make a new word. The prefixes 'un' and 'dis' make a word with its opposite meaning.
5 **undo**
6 **unfortunate**
7 **disobeyed**
8 **unkind**
9 **unsure**
10 **dislike**
11–12 Two sentences, one written in the past (something that has already happened) and one in the present (something happening now).
13–16 Homophones are words that sound the same but are spelled differently and have different meanings.
13 **where**
14 **whole**
15 **know**
16 **shore**
17 Commas sit between items in a list. When we went swimming we had to remember a **towel, drink, swimming costume, brush and goggles.**

18–21 Apostrophes for contraction show where letters are missed out of a word. In each case here the apostrophe shows where the 'o' has been removed from the word 'not'.
18 **mustn't**
19 **haven't**
20 **wasn't**
21 **shouldn't**
22 e
23 l
24 w
25 i
26 j
27 r
28–30 An adjective is a word used to describe somebody or something.
28 Tuhil has the longest legs.
29 Gemma is the youngest at the party.
30 Dan's story is shorter than Mia's.
31–33 The helper verbs 'is' and 'are' are from the verb 'to be'.
31 Ten children **are** playing on the climbing frame.
32 Lucy **is** going to Arwa's house for tea.
33 Adele and Harvey **are** going on holiday.
34–37 Compound words are words made from two shorter words that are put together.
34 **bedroom**
35 **haircut**
36 **sunflower**
37 **eyebrow**
38 *quickly*
39 *jump*
40 *unhappy*
41 *unwell*
42 *shout*
43 *sleepy*

Mixed Paper 5 (pages 64–69)

1 **a**
2 **b**
3 **eleven weeks**
4 *for food and protection*
5–8 Words that start with the following letters:
5 **g** *girl*
6 **k** *kite*
7 **p** *puppy*
8 **v** *vet*
9 A statement sentence gives information. *The teacher is calling in the children.*
10 A question sentence asks a question. *Why is the teacher calling in the children?*
11 An exclamation sentence expresses strong feeling. *Quickly come in!*
12 A command sentence tells someone to do something. *Come in now because it is raining.*
13 **swan**
14 **watch**
15 **wash**
16 Remember, If the word ends with a consonant + 'y' the 'y' is changed to an 'i' and the suffix is added.

	+ er	+ est
smoky	smokier	smokiest
cloudy	**cloudier**	**cloudiest**
creaky	**creakier**	**creakiest**
smelly	**smellier**	**smelliest**

17–19 Look out for apostrophes for contraction and for possession. See keywords on pages 79–80 for their definitions.
17 **Mia's** brother went shopping but **didn't** like it.
18 It **hasn't** been this cold for a long time.
19 **Jacob's** coat fell on the floor.
20 *pedal signal*
21 *fossil nostril*
22 A soft c sounds like an 's' in the word. **city centre ice**
23–25 An adverb tells us *how* something is done, *when* something is done or *where* something is done.
23 I left my game downstairs. **where**
24 Yesterday we went to see the circus. **when**
25 We slowly walked home after school. **how**
26–29 A pronoun is a word used in place of a noun.
26 **He** looked at **me** with surprise.
27 When can **I** come home?
28 **They** are **mine**.
29 **She** really liked **his** story.
30 **many**
31 **great**
32 **water**
33 **after**

Mixed Paper 6 (pages 70–75)

1. c
2. c
3. *clever, confident, assured*
4. Answers about how George must have had a tiring week because he had been crying so much, or perhaps because he works so hard to be clever.
5. **televishun** should be spelled television
6. **muther** should be spelled mother
7. **meny** should be spelled many
8. **tresure** should be spelled treasure

9–10 Adding the prefix 'un' or 'dis' changes the word into its opposite meaning.

9. *unpack undo*
10. *disappear dislike*

11–13 Capital letters are needed for the beginning of a sentence, proper nouns and the word 'I'. Punctuation is needed at the end of each of these sentences. Commas are needed between items listed in a sentence.

11. **T**his morning **C**lare asked if she could come to my house.
12. **S**hall **I** bring my pillow, sleeping bag and tent**?**
13. **O**n **M**onday **I** am going on holiday.
14. beautiful
15. father
16. behind
17. improve
18. A soft g sounds like an 'j' in the word. *giant, giraffe, cage, orange, gym*

19–22 The helper verbs 'was' and 'were' are from the verb 'to be'.

19. The dog **was** walking on the lead.
20. The children **were** riding the ponies.
21. Leena **was** cooking a cake.
22. We **were** going to go to the zoo but it is raining.

23–25 A conjunction is a joining word. The sentences must include the given conjunctions.

26–29 Alphabetical order is the order the initial letters of the word are placed in the alphabet.

26. **crawl**
27. **run**
28. **swim**
29. **walk**
30. station
31. motion
32. fiction
33. direction

34–37 The beginning of each sentence gives a clue as to which is the correct order.

34. **Once upon a time a king lost his crown.**
35. **While he was searching, he found his glasses.**
36. **Then he found the robe he lost last year.**
37. **In the end he found his crown, it was in the bathroom!**

Puzzle 2 (page 76)

1. **five**
2. **accidents, bones**
3. *Dogs*
4. **j, o**

Notes